My Life Belongs to Jesus
New Believer Handbook

War Room Nations // Ministry Resources

My Life Belongs to Jesus

Before I was saved, I was a liar, a cheater, and a thief. I did drugs and drank alcohol every day. For a brief time, I even worked for the Mexican cartel running illegal immigrants across the southern border into the United States.

I hurt people emotionally and physically. I used women for pleasure and was addicted to self-mutilation. I was full of pride and lived for the party. The definition of selfishness does not even begin to describe the kind of person that I was.

Even after having kids of my own, when I thought I could change, things continued to get worse.

I was a horrible husband and father; I took advantage of everyone that was in my life and did not care about anyone but myself. I did what I wanted, when I wanted, and no one could tell me otherwise.

Do not even get me started on what I thought about Christians. I grew up around that stuff. My grandparents were pastors of a church. I saw the hypocrisy in people. It was all fake to me. To me religion was full of nothing but hypocrites. There was no way that I would ever give God a chance.

Then, in 2016, after 18 years of addiction & sin, when I had burned every bridge, lost my job, had two felonies against me, and had no friends left to party with, I finally came to the end of myself.

I fell to my knees and told God, *"I give up. If you really have a purpose for my life, then let's try things your way."*

At that very moment, I felt His undeniable presence come into the room, and everything changed! I was saved and radically transformed by the power of God.

Soon after, I invested my life to share the gospel and seek the lost. This is the great commission of Jesus.

I carry a deep conviction to tell others about the good news of salvation, and I use God's gifting in my life to teach, train, and equip others in their own calling.

I am so excited that you are holding this book in your hands! It means that you made the greatest decision of your life!

Friend, I want you to know that if everything I went through in my life was for the sole purpose that you would be reading this book today, it was worth it.

Welcome to the family!

Evangelist Armando Perez

TABLE OF CONTENTS

11. What is church?

12. What are my rights as a family member?

13. What is baptism + Do I need to be baptized?

14. What is communion?

15. What happens when I die?

16. What about?

17. What do I do next?

WHAT HAPPENED WHEN I RECEIVED THE LIFE OF CHRIST?

When you receive the life of Christ, you are receiving a gift that was always yours to receive. It is the realization that you finally accept and believe what God has always believed about you. We call this *faith*. God sees you as pure, clean, and accepted because Jesus took care of all your sins when He took everyone's sins to the cross.

FOR IT IS BY GRACE YOU HAVE BEEN SAVED, THROUGH FAITH AND THIS IS NOT FROM YOURSELVES, IT IS THE GIFT OF GOD. [EPHESIANS 2:8 NIV]

CHRIST, HOWEVER, OFFERED ONE SACRIFICE FOR SINS, AN OFFERING THAT IS EFFECTIVE FOREVER, AND THEN HE SAT DOWN AT THE RIGHT SIDE OF GOD. ... WITH ONE SACRIFICE, THEN, HE HAS MADE PERFECT FOREVER THOSE WHO ARE PURIFIED FROM SIN. [HEBREWS 10:12 & 14 GNT]

You are loved by the Father, and He is pleased with you. When God the Father looks at you, He does not see your past mistakes or failures. He does not judge you for anything you have done.

He only sees Christ in you, and you now have a right standing with Him because of Jesus.

BY FAITH WE HAVE BEEN MADE ACCEPTABLE TO GOD. AND NOW, THANKS TO OUR LORD JESUS CHRIST, WE HAVE PEACE WITH GOD. CHRIST HAS ALSO INTRODUCED US TO GOD'S GIFT OF UNDESERVED GRACE ON WHICH WE NOW TAKE OUR STAND.
[ROMANS 5:1-2 CEV]

God sees you this way because when Jesus died on the cross, He died as you and for you. He died for all your sins for all time. He took all the punishment so that you do not have to. Here is what God says about you.

> ➤ In Christ you are completely loved by God.

Long ago the Lord said to Israel: "I have loved you, my people, with an everlasting love. With unfailing love I have drawn you to myself. [Jeremiah 31:3 NLT]

For this is how God loved the world: He gave his one and only Son, so that everyone who believes in him will not perish but have eternal life. [John 3:16 NLT]

See how very much our Father loves us, for he calls us his children, and that is what we are! But the people who belong to this world don't recognize that we are God's children because they don't know him. ... We know what real love is because Jesus gave up his life for us. So we also ought to give up our lives for our brothers and sisters. [1 John 3:1 & 16 NLT]

➢ You are a trophy of Christ's victory.
God calls you a "saint."

*But thank God! He has made us his captives
and continues to lead us along in Christ's
triumphal procession. Now he uses us to spread the
knowledge of Christ everywhere, like a sweet
perfume. [2 Corinthians 2:14 NLT]*

*Always thanking the Father. He has enabled you to
share in the inheritance that belongs to his people,
who live in the light. [Colossians 1:12 NLT]*

➢ You are a new creation, completely forgiven and
made righteous in Christ.

*This means that anyone who belongs to Christ
has become a new person. The old life is gone, a
new life has begun! … For God made Christ, who
never sinned, to be the offering for our sin,
so that we could be made right with God through
Christ. [2 Corinthians 5:17 & 21 NLT]*

*He is so rich in kindness and grace that he purchased
our freedom with the blood of his Son and forgave our
sins. He has showered his kindness on us, along with
all wisdom and understanding. [Ephesians 1:7-8 NLT]*

*We are made right with God by placing our faith in
Jesus Christ. And this is true for everyone who
believes, no matter who we are. [Romans 3:22 NLT]*

> You are a child of God, and He delights in you.

See how very much our Father loves us, for he calls us his children, and that is what we are! But the people who belong to this world don't recognize that we are God's children because they don't know him. [1 John 3:1 NLT]

> You are one with the Lord Jesus and the temple or home of the Holy Spirit.

Since we have been united with him in his death, we will also be raised to life as he was. We know that our old sinful selves were crucified with Christ so that sin might lose its power in our lives. We are no longer slaves to sin. For when we died with Christ we were set free from the power of sin. [Romans 6:5-7 NLT]

Don't you realize that your body is the temple of the Holy Spirit, who lives in you and was given to you by God? You do not belong to yourself. [1 Corinthians 6:19 NLT]

> You are blameless and holy.

Some of you were once like that. But you were cleansed; you were made holy; you were made right with God by calling on the name of the Lord Jesus Christ and by the Spirit of our God. [1 Corinthians 6:11 NLT]

For God made Christ, who never sinned, to be the offering for our sin, so that we could be made right with God through Christ. [2 Corinthians 5:21 NLT]

- ➢ You are a joint heir adopted into the family of Jesus Christ.

And since we are his children, we are his heirs. In fact, together with Christ we are heirs of God's glory. But if we are to share his glory, we must also share his suffering. [Romans 8:17 NLT]

WHO IS GOD?

We read in Genesis (the first book of the Bible) that God created everything - light, earth, water, air, plants, animals, and humans. God created the entire world out of nothing and everything that God created, God called "good." God saved the best for the last day of creation; he created people in His own image.

In the beginning, everyone and everything was created good. All of it was created to reflect the glory of God. This has not changed. All of creation is still meant to reflect God's glory.

God exists as three distinct persons that the New Testament refers to as the Father, the Son, and the Holy Spirit. God reveals Himself to us as three distinct persons that are also *one in unity.*

So, God is *one in unity* but *three in diversity.*

Historically, Christians refer to this as the <u>Trinity</u> or <u>Triune God</u>.

Each one - Father, Son (Jesus) and Spirit *is God.*

Together they are God.

The name first used for God in the Old Testament is *'Elohim.'* It comes from the Hebrew root meaning "strength" or "power," and it has the unusual characteristic of being plural in form. There are many names used to describe God in the Bible.

WHO IS THE FATHER?

God the Father is the same God that the Hebrew people in the Old Testament understood as God.
The Supreme Creator of heaven and earth.

Because the nature of God is beyond our ability to understand, Jesus taught us to think of God as our Father so that we could better understand God's loving character.

The Bible tells us that God loves us with an endless love.

**I HAVE LOVED YOU WITH AN EVERLASTING LOVE.
[JEREMIAH 31:3 NIV]**

**SEE WHAT GREAT LOVE THE FATHER HAS LAVISHED ON US, THAT WE SHOULD BE CALLED CHILDREN OF GOD! AND THAT IS WHAT WE ARE.
[1 JOHN 3:1 NIV]**

WHO IS JESUS CHRIST?

God the Son (Jesus Christ) is the person of God that came to earth in human form to live as one of us.

In His human form, His earthly parents named Him 'Yeshua' (Hebrew) or Jesus (Greek) that comes from the Hebrew word for "savior."

The term "Christ" is Jesus' divine title, and it means "chosen one."

Because He is God but came to earth as man, He can identify with us and we with Him. He is equal to God the Father but identifies as a son so that we can better understand Him.

> ➢ He was pre-existent with the Father.

He existed in the beginning with God. God created everything through him, and nothing was created except through him. [John 1:2-3 NLT]

Now, Father, bring me into the glory we shared before the world began. [John 17:5 NLT]

He existed before anything else, and he holds all creation together. [Colossians 1:17 NLT]

> ➢ He was sinless, as only God can be and He forgives sin, as only God can.

- ➤ He accomplished the works of His father by fulfilling the law given by God to His people, and He fulfilled biblical prophecy spoken about the Messiah (*anointed one, expected king*).

- ➤ He died on the Cross as the ransom for our sins, but on the third day He was resurrected from the dead. This is the fundamental theme of the Gospel.

- ➤ He is a personal savior.

If you openly declare that Jesus is Lord and believe in your heart that God raised him from the dead, you will be saved. For it is by believing in your heart that you are made right with God, and it is by openly declaring your faith that you are saved. [Romans 10:9-10 NLT]

WHO IS THE HOLY SPIRIT?

God the Holy Spirit is the person of God that exists in the world as spirit. He lives in us and when we receive the life of Christ by faith, the Holy Spirit gives us power to live out our new identity in this world.

The Holy Spirit is a beautiful and powerful part of who God is. We need Him in our life as a conduit to become who God created us to be, and through His power we have aid in all situations. Without Him, we are powerless.

Our first encounter with the Holy Spirit is when He convicts us of our sin, shows us that none of us can live up to the righteousness of Jesus, and reveals to us the judgment that is coming to those who die without a Savior.

AND WHEN HE COMES, HE WILL CONVICT THE WORLD OF ITS SIN, AND OF GOD'S RIGHTEOUSNESS, AND OF THE COMING JUDGEMENT. THE WORLD'S SIN IS THAT IT REFUSES TO BELIEVE IN ME. RIGHTEOUSNESS IS AVAILABLE BECAUSE I GO TO THE FATHER, AND YOU WILL SEE ME NO MORE. JUDGEMENT WILL COME BECAUSE THE RULER OF THIS WORLD HAS ALREADY BEEN JUDGED. [JOHN 16:8-11 NLT]

As we repent, confess our sins, and receive the gift of salvation the Holy Spirit regenerates our dead inner human spirit which now becomes sensitive to the spiritual things of God.

JESUS REPLIED, "I ASSURE YOU NO ONE CAN ENTER THE KINGDOM OF GOD WITHOUT BEING BORN OF WATER AND THE SPIRIT. HUMANS CAN REPRODUCE ONLY HUMAN LIFE, BUT THE HOLY SPIRIT GIVES BIRTH TO SPIRITUAL LIFE. SO DON'T BE SURPRISED WHEN I SAY, 'YOU MUST BE BORN AGAIN.' THE WIND BLOWS WHEREVER IT WANTS. JUST AS YOU CAN HEAR THE WIND BUT CAN'T TELL WHERE IT COMES FROM OR WHERE IT IS GOING, SO YOU CAN'T EXPLAIN HOW PEOPLE ARE BORN OF THE SPIRIT," [JOHN 3:5-8 NLT]

PETER REPLIED, "EACH OF YOU MUST REPENT OF YOUR SINS AND TURN TO GOD, AND BE BAPTIZED IN THE NAME OF JESUS CHRIST FOR THE FORGIVENESS OF YOUR SINS. THEN YOU WILL RECEIVE THE GIFT OF THE HOLY SPIRIT. [ACTS 2:38 NLT]

There is a second work of the Holy Spirit when He baptizes a believer. It is available to all and a gift of empowerment, helping the believer to live a holy life. Through the power of the Holy Spirit "the Helper" we become more like Jesus and are directed to do the Father's will.

Furthermore, the gift is primarily for the empowerment to witness to others.

AND EVERYONE PRESENT WAS FILLED WITH THE HOLY SPIRIT AND BEGAN SPEAKING IN OTHER LANGUAGES, AS THE HOLY SPIRIT GAVE THEM THIS ABILITY. [ACTS 2:4 NLT]

THIS PROMISE IS TO YOU, TO YOUR CHILDREN, AND TO THOSE FAR AWAY- ALL WHO HAVE BEEN CALLED BY THE LORD OUR GOD. [ACTS 2:39 NLT]

BUT YOU WILL RECEIVE POWER WHEN THE HOLY SPIRIT COMES UPON YOU. AND YOU WILL BE MY WITNESSES, TELLING PEOPLE ABOUT ME EVERYWHERE – IN JERUSALEM, THROUGHOUT JUDEA, IN SAMARIA, AND TO THE ENDS OF THE EARTH. [ACTS 1:8 NLT]

We are encouraged to ask the Holy Spirit to fill us up on a regular basis. When you feel depleted or need strength, ask Him to replenish you.

DON'T BE DRUNK WITH WINE, BECAUSE THAT WILL RUIN YOUR LIFE, INSTEAD, BE FILLED WITH THE HOLY SPIRIT. [EPHESIANS 5:18 NLT]

WHY DO I NEED A SAVIOR?

The Bible teaches that because of Adam's disobedience in thinking he could be "as God" by knowing good and evil, sin entered the world that we all live in.

In the Bible, the word "sin" means to "miss the mark." Adam missed the mark. He was deceived when he believed that knowing good and evil would make him like God. He chose the tree of morality instead of the tree of life. Knowing good and evil revealed to Adam his nakedness and how much he was *not like God.*

God removed him from the garden so that he could not then choose to eat from the tree of life, protecting humanity from being forever stuck in that knowledge with no way to repair the relationship.

THEN THE LORD GOD SAID, "LOOK, THE HUMAN BEINGS HAVE BECOME LIKE US, KNOWING BOTH GOOD AND EVIL. WHAT IF THEY REACH OUT, TAKE FRUIT FROM THE TREE OF LIFE, AND EAT IT? THEN THEY WILL LIVE FOREVER!" SO THE LORD GOD BANISHED THEM FROM THE GARDEN OF EDEN, AND HE SENT ADAM OUT TO CULTIVATE THE GROUND FROM WHICH HE HAD BEEN MADE.
[GENESIS 3:22-23 NLT]

In Romans 3:23, Paul says, **"For everyone has sinned; we all fall short of God's glorious standard."**

But in the very next verse, he says, "***Yet God, with undeserved kindness, declares that we are righteous [back in right relationship with God]. He did this through Christ Jesus when He freed us from the penalty for our sins. For God presented Jesus as the sacrifice for sin.***

People are made right with God when they believe that Jesus sacrificed His life, shedding His blood. This sacrifice shows that God was being fair when He held back and did not punish those who sinned in times past, for He was looking ahead and including them in what He would do in this present time.

God did this to demonstrate His righteousness, for He Himself is fair and just, and He declares sinners to be right in His sight when they believe in Jesus. [Romans 3:24-26 NLT]

Jesus restored our ability to choose life.

"I came so everyone would have life and have it fully." [John 10:10 CEV]

WHAT IS THE BIBLE + HOW DO I READ IT?

The Bible is the word of God revealed throughout history to point humanity to Jesus. The Holy Spirit uses the Bible to show us Jesus and reveal the Father's plan to have a relationship with you. In the Old Testament, the understanding about Jesus is hidden in the message to the Jewish people. In the New Testament, the understanding about Jesus is exposed in the message to the believers.

Bible basics: There are sixty-six books, written down by a total of over 35 Holy Spirit inspired authors across 1500 years and three continents. While Genesis (the first book) talks about the beginning and Revelation (the last book) tells us of the victory in the end, the books are not in chronological order. Instead, they are grouped by subject - Books of the Law, History, Poetry, Prophets, Gospels, and Epistles.

The *Old Testament* is God's written word to the Jewish people to reveal to the world its need for a savior after Adam's disobedience.

The *Gospels* are the first four books of the New Testament written on the life and teachings of Jesus.

The *Book of Acts* is the history of the beginnings of the church.

The rest of the *New Testament* books reveal the new covenant that Jesus made with God on our behalf to put us back in right relationship with God.

Here is a suggestion of where to start:

- **The Gospel of John** - ('Gospel' means good news) In this book, John tells you about God's love for us and why Jesus came.

- **Ephesians** - Ephesians is an 'epistle' (a fancy word for a letter written by Paul to the church in the city of Ephesus) In Ephesians, Paul shows us how the Gospel affects our everyday lives. It also shows us how it was God's plan to create a multi-ethnic and racially diverse community in His church.

- **Romans** - In this epistle, written to the believers in Rome, Paul shows us that Jesus created a new covenant or 'legal agreement' with God that makes us family through His death, resurrection and by sending the Holy Spirit to us. This book more deeply explains God's love and that the work of Jesus completely took care of our sins. All we need to do is believe, have faith, and to receive the life He now gives us.

Free Bible App Download:

YouVersion

bible.com/app

WHAT IS THE GOSPEL?

The fullest meaning of the word Gospel is *the good news.* It declares that because Jesus took care of our sins by dying on the cross, we do not have to do anything other than receive the gift of life He's given to us.

It allows us to simply live out our new identity in Christ as a child of God.

You have been forgiven of your sins, given a brand-new life to live, and have the eternal promise of a life with Jesus.

WHAT DOES GRACE MEAN?

Grace is God's unmerited favor toward us because of what Jesus did for us. Grace is revealed in the person of Jesus.

In our lives, grace means that we do not have to keep revisiting all the things we have done wrong and make amends for them to make God pleased with us. Jesus already did that.

Instead, His Spirit lives in and through us. As you relax into that knowledge, grace will influence your thoughts and decisions.

FOR GOD HAS REVEALED HIS GRACE FOR THE SALVATION OF ALL PEOPLE. THAT GRACE INSTRUCTS US TO GIVE UP UNGODLY LIVING AND WORLDLY PASSIONS, AND TO LIVE SELF-CONTROLLED, UPRIGHT, AND GODLY LIVES IN THIS WORLD, AS WE WAIT FOR THE BLESSED DAY WE HOPE FOR, WHEN THE GLORY OF OUR GREAT GOD AND SAVIOR JESUS CHRIST WILL APPEAR. HE GAVE HIMSELF FOR US, TO RESCUE US FROM ALL WICKEDNESS AND TO MAKE US A PURE PEOPLE WHO BELONG TO HIM ALONE AND ARE EAGER TO DO GOOD. [TITUS 2:11-14 GNT]

WHAT HAPPENS IF I DO SOMETHING WRONG?

If you do something wrong, the bible clearly tells us we must repent.

Understand that the Bible word translated "repent" means to change the way you think, or to "rethink" what you have done within your new identity in Christ.

It is important to know that doing something wrong does not disqualify you from your new identity in Christ. It simply means that your mind (also called your "soul" in the Bible) has old pathways of understanding that need to change.

As you begin to understand who you truly are in God's eyes, the desire to commit sin or do wrong, hurtful, or harmful things naturally falls away.

Don't copy the behavior and customs of this world, but let God transform you into a new person by changing the way you think. Then you will learn to know God's will for you, which is good and pleasing and perfect. [Romans 12:2 NLT]

You need to begin to "renew your mind." That is, you need to change how you think.

Beginning to think the way Jesus would think, and starting to believe about yourself the same things God believes about you, comes from spending time reading and hearing what God says.

That is why we read and study the Bible, and why it is a vital part of every Christian's journey to get rooted in a local church of believers that will gather to learn and grow each week.

WHAT IS CHURCH?

The local church is where we do life together.

God established the church on earth as His perfect will for His family. It is the primary place that we learn about our new life and where we grow in knowledge about our relationship with God. It is where we grow with other members of God's family.

> ➤ It is where we develop our gifts as sons and daughters.

> ➤ It is where we find strength and encouragement when we need help.

> ➤ It is where we learn how to share our new life with others.

> ➤ It is the means that God uses to make His love and grace known in the world.

Consistent and frequent gathering with a local church to hear the good news of God's grace is a vital component to living your fullest life. The church is important to God. It is so important to God, that He calls us the bride of Jesus. The church is not a building, it is a people unified as one body.

WHAT ARE MY RIGHTS AS A FAMILY MEMBER?

Because Christ has already done for us everything needed to be in right-standing with God, we do not need to do anything to prove that.

However, when we receive the life of Christ, we take our place as part of the family of God. *As family members*, we share in the common needs and life of the family.

As a follower of Jesus, He asks that we love God and love people. We do this by following Christ's example to serve one another. We serve God's family for the same reason we serve in our own home & family.

It is important that we never forget the grace God gave to us when we were sinners. Now we continue to be thankful for our salvation and seek to share the good news with others that they might know Jesus as their personal savior too. We do this through our generosity in giving and our participation or service within God's family (the church).

WHAT IS BAPTISM + DO I NEED TO BE BAPTIZED?

The Bible teaches that all new believers were baptized. It symbolizes burying your old life with Christ and being born into a new life. Your past is not a horrible memory that God still holds on to. To God, your past no longer matters at all. He chooses to no longer remember your sins or hold them against you.

And I will forgive their wickedness, and I will never again remember their sins. [Hebrews 8:12 NLT]

Paul tells us in Romans that we are married (in union) with Christ. Meaning that we were co-crucified, co-buried, co-resurrected and we now co-reign with Christ. So, as you go under the water, see it as a picture of what took place on the cross - old things passed away and now you have a new life in Christ!

Jesus tells us the importance of baptism in the book of John.

Jesus replied, "I assure you; no one can enter the Kingdom of God without being born of water and the Spirit. [John 3:5 NLT]

WHAT IS COMMUNION?

The word "communion" means _common union_ or _unity in being together_.

The Bible says that Jesus ate a meal with His disciples on the night before His death to reveal to them that the Old Covenant (the agreement God made with Abraham) was ending. He was making a New Covenant with them that would be for all people and His death would finally take care of their sins.

We take communion together to remember, rejoice, and to celebrate being joined with Him.

We do this regularly to remind us of what Jesus has done for us, and in remembrance of the power that is in the death, burial, and resurrection of Christ.

It is the perfect representation of the His life now being in us. Bread represents His body, and the drink represents His blood.

WHAT HAPPENS WHEN I DIE?

The Bible teaches that when we die, our soul (the conscious part of us) immediately joins the presence of Christ.

So we are always confident, even though we know that as long as we live in these bodies we are not at home with the Lord. For we live by believing and not by seeing. Yes, we are fully confident, and we would rather be away from these earthly bodies, for then we will be at home with the Lord. [2 Corinthians 5:6-8 NLT]

If you find yourself fearful of death and expectant of a coming judgment in your life, you have not been properly introduced to Jesus Christ and the mission He accomplished while here in the earth. The truth is, when you trust in Christ's death it instantaneously becomes your death, His burial becomes your burial, and His resurrection is also your resurrection!

Jesus' purpose for living was not only to come *for you* but to come *as you.* He came to take your place on the cross so that you could share in His place with the Father.

- o He was rejected so that you could be accepted.

- o He was hated so that you could be loved.

- o He was despised so that you could be distinguished.

o   He was tortured so that you could be made whole.

The sin of the world was placed upon Him so that we could be forgiven, filled with life, and made completely right in God's eyes. This exchange gives us access to a fear-free life of rest and peace.

Simply believe in what Jesus did for you and receive all the joy He has provided for you to share in this amazing life!

WHAT ABOUT...?

Misinterpretation often leads to troubling questions. You may be wondering about the following concerns based on misinformation about what Jesus did for us on the cross.

> ➤ **DO WE NEED TO FOCUS ON OVERCOMING OUR SIN?**

No! God does not condemn us for our sins once He has forgiven them. The cross has obliterated them. Our own efforts are useless without the power of the Holy Spirit. As we walk in our new identity, the Holy Spirit will begin to lead us to walk out a life that is pure and more like Christ.

So now there is no condemnation for those who belong to Christ Jesus. And because you belong to him, the power of the life-giving Spirit has freed you from the power of sin that leads to death. [Romans 8:1 NLT]

> ➤ **DO WE REALLY HAVE TO FORGIVE AND FORGET?**

The truth is that in our new nature we will come to forgive others, but it is not true that we will forget. Forgiveness is for our healing. We intentionally choose to release the person from our anger. Do not dwell on the past and do not hold grudges.

Instead, be kind to each other, tenderhearted, forgiving one another, just as God through Christ has forgiven you. [Ephesians 4:32 NLT]

> ## ➤ DO WE GROW IN HOLINESS?

No! Holiness is the act of God setting us apart for His own purpose. It is not something we do, rather it is an act of grace that God does through the Holy Spirit.

Growth in Christ is not achieving a status. We have already received the fullness of Christ in salvation. Growing is the renewing of the mind to understand that God has already made us holy.

God has united you with Christ Jesus. For our benefit God made him to be wisdom itself. Christ made us right with God; he made us pure and holy, and he freed us from sin. [1 Corinthians 1:30 NLT]

> ## ➤ CAN OUR SINS DISQUALIFY US FROM BEING USED BY GOD?

No! There is no sin you can ever commit that is able to undo the work of Christ.

If we are unfaithful, he remains faithful, for he cannot deny who he is. [2 Timothy 2:13 NLT]

➢ ARE OUR SINS COVERED BY THE BLOOD OF JESUS?

No! Jesus completely did away with our sins, He did not cover them up.

And you know that Jesus came to take away our sins, and there is no sin in him. [1 John 3:5 NLT]

WHAT DO I DO NEXT?

You do not need to do anything to maintain who you are in Christ. You are beloved, so _be loved!_

Go out and live life more abundantly with your new DNA which is your new nature as a child of God the Father.

You are part of a new family, God's family!

We celebrate your decision to follow Jesus!

**In the same way, there is more joy in heaven over one lost sinner who repents and returns to God than over ninety-nine others who are righteous and haven't strayed away! [Luke 15:7 NLT]**

I encourage you to connect with a local church in your city. If you do not have a local church, I invite you to email my contact address at the end of this book.

Tell someone else about your new faith in Christ, and more importantly, spend time with God each day through prayer and Bible reading.

Thank you for reading this book. Let us know about the decision you made and how this book has impacted you. We are rejoicing with you!

Armando Perez
Contact: aperezbooks@outlook.com

Cover layout by Jenn Foster - eliteonlinepublishing.com

Written by Armando Perez